How Do Lions Say I Love You?

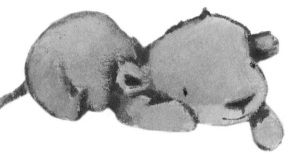

By Diane Muldrow
Illustrated by David Walker

A GOLDEN BOOK • NEW YORK

Text copyright © 2009 by Diane E. Muldrow
Illustrations copyright © 2009 by David Walker
All rights reserved.
Published in the United States by Golden Books, an imprint of Random House Children's Books,
a division of Random House, Inc., 1745 Broadway, New York, NY 10019.
Originally published in different form in the United States by Golden Books, New York, in 2009.
Golden Books, A Golden Book, A Little Golden Book, the G colophon, and
the distinctive gold spine are registered trademarks of Random House, Inc.
randomhouse.com/kids
Educators and librarians, for a variety of teaching tools, visit us at RHTeachersLibrarians.com
Library of Congress Control Number: 2012943918
ISBN 978-0-449-81256-3
Printed in the United States of America
10 9 8 7 6 5 4 3 2 1

A hen says *I love you*
to her chicks with a cluck.

Swans mate for life
'cause they're truly love-struck.

Giraffes say *I love you*
with their necks so long.

The nightingale sings
it in a beautiful song.

The peacock says *I love you*
with his feathers and flair.

Horses say *I love you*
by sharing their air.

Elephants hug
in their own
special way.

"I'm here, my dear,"
is what they seem to say.

Lions say *I love you*
with a purr and a cuddle.

Wolves say *I love you*
with a howl and a huddle.

Bears like to say it
with a kiss on the muzzle.

A mama cow says it
with a lick and a nuzzle.

Mourning doves like
to bill and coo.
And that's how they
say *I love you*.